AUSTRALIAN – ENGLISH
ENGLISH – AUSTRALIAN

Compiled by
ANTHEA BICKERTON

D0551815

**ABSON
BOOKS
LONDON** 5 Sidney Square London E1 2EY England

ABSON BOOKS LONDON
5 Sidney Square London E1 2EY England

First published in Great Britain, August 1976
Second Edition March 1988
11th impression November 2006

Compiled and edited by Anthea Bickerton
© Anthea Bickerton and Pat McCormack
Cover design by Chris Bird

Printed by Gutenberg Press, Malta
ISBN 0 902920 71 5 (10 digits)
ISBN 978 0 902920 71 2 (13 digits)

PREFACE

To catch the essence of any country it is helpful to know what the natives are talking about. We all know that Australians speak *English* but many words in common use are *foreign* to us, and cannot be guessed at. "A real breath of Australia' was how someone described the First Edition of this glossary. When it was compiled in the seventies the people who used it were mainly immigrants and those with relatives in Australia. "It helps me to keep in touch" said one bereft Wolverhampton grandmother.

Now there is a stampede for holidays and business towards the world's largest island and smallest continent, 25 times the size of Great Britain and Ireland.

I am indebted to my team, too many to name, composed of new Australians, old Australians and Brits who have lived and worked there.

Further suggestions will always be welcomed.

Anthea Bickerton

CONTENTS

	AUSTRALIAN	ENGLISH
A	**Abo/Aborigine**	native Australian
	ANZAC	Australia and New Zealand Army Corps
	Anzac(s)	soldier(s)
	Apple-islander *(colloq.)*	Tasmanian resident
	arvo	afternoon
	ABC	Australian Broadcasting Corporation ('Aunty')
	ASIO *(pron. AZIO)*	Australian Security and Intelligence Organisation
	Aussie	Australia/Australian
	Aussie rules	football (Australian code)
	award rate	minimum rate of pay
B	**backblocks**	remote country
	back of Bourke	back of beyond
	back yard	back garden
	banana bender *(colloq.)*	Queenslander
	barbie	barbeque

AUSTRALIAN	ENGLISH
barrack (for) *(v.)*	support *(sports, etc.)*
beanie	woolly hat
beaut(y)	great/marvellous
beef road	road for trucking *(qv)* cattle by road train *(qv)*
bell *(give someone a)*	ring/telephone/call
billabong	pond
billy	can/tin for boiling water
bindyi	prickle
block *(of land)*	plot *(of land)*
blowfly	bluebottle
bludger	lazy person
bluebottle	type of jellyfish
bonzer	good/great
boomer	large kangaroo/anything big
boomerang	Aboriginal hunting weapon/any article that will be returned
bottle shop	off-licence
bowser	petrol pump

AUSTRALIAN	ENGLISH
brown coal	soft coal
brumby	wild horse
buck's night/buck's party	stag party
bull dust	fine dust found on outback *(qv)* roads/bullshit *(colloq.)*
bundi	rock
bungalow	single-storey holiday cottage
bunyip	mythical creature
bush *(go)*	live rough in the countryside
bush *(the)*	the countryside
bushed	lost/tired
bushfly	fly *(smaller than blowfly)*
bushman	one who understands living in the bush
bushranger	highwayman
bushwalker	hiker
bushwhacker	country person
BYO *(bring your own)*	supply own drinks for restaurant/party

C

AUSTRALIAN	ENGLISH
Captain Cook *(have a)*	have a look
cark-it	die
carry on *(v)*	lark about
Centre *(the)*	Central Australia
check *(to pass in one's)*	die
chips *(potato)*	crisps
chook	chicken
chunder *(v.)*	vomit/to be sick
clapped out	worthless
claypan	dried out pond/lake bed
cobber	friend
cocky	a small farmer
coloured pencil	crayon
come good	turn out right
comfort station	toilet
Commonwealth *(usually refers to Australian Federation of States)*	Commonwealth *(usually refers to British Commonwealth of Nations)*
compo	compensation

AUSTRALIAN	ENGLISH
contraceptive	condom/Durex *(brand name)*
cordial	fruit squash
cove	chap/fellow
cozzy	swimsuit
creek	occasional stream
crook	sick/ill/out of order
Cross, The *(or Kings)*	nightclub/redlight area of Sydney
crow eater *(colloq.)*	South Australian

D

dag	matted sheep turd/term of endearment or mild abuse
dam *(agric.)*	pond/reservoir
damper	bread without yeast cooked in ashes of camp fire
dead ringer for	spitting image of
deli	foodshop
didgeridoo	Aboriginal musical instrument made from hollowed stem of tree
digger	Australian soldier

AUSTRALIAN	ENGLISH
dill	idiot
dingo	Australian wild dog
dinkum	genuine/honest
dirt road	unsurfaced road
dob someone in	drop someone in it
dogger	dingo hunter
draft	conscription
drapes	curtains
drongo	worthless person/idiot
dry *(the)*	dry season in the Tropics
duco	paintwork *(on cars, etc.)*
duds	best clothes
dunny	toilet
durex	sellotape
eggplant	aubergine
emu-bob	a session picking up litter
esky	portable ice box

E

	AUSTRALIAN	ENGLISH
F	fibro	asbestos board
	financial	paid up/solvent/in the black
	fire plug	fire hydrant
	flake	shark meat
	flash-flood	sudden storm flood
	floater/pie floater	meat pie soup
	footy	Australian Rules – football
	fossick	have a look around
	frankfurts	frankfurters
	freeway	motorway
	full	drunk
G	galah	parrot/idiot
	galvo	galvanised iron
	gander	look closely
	garbo	dustman
	gin	Aboriginal woman
	give away *(v.)*	to give up
	give someone heaps	wind someone up *(colloq.)*

AUSTRALIAN	ENGLISH
globe *(light)*	bulb
goanna	lizard *(very large)*
G'day	Good morning/afternoon/evening
good oil	information
good on ya	well done/good for you
gravel road	unmetalled road
grazier	farmer *(on land owned by himself)*
grouse	great
guernsey	jersey/sports shirt
guernsey *(to get a)*	to get a place in a team
gum boots	wellingtons/gum boots
gum tree	eucalyptus tree
get off my back	leave me alone

hook *(v.)*	steal
hotel	pub
hot-water bag	hot-water bottle
hot-water service	immersion heater
how're you going?	how are you?
humpy	shanty/shack

	AUSTRALIAN	ENGLISH
I	**icy pole**	ice lolly
	incorporated *(company)*	limited/plc
	intersection *(road)*	junction
	interstate	to or from another State
J	**jackeroo**	male pupil on sheep/cattle station
	jacked *(off)*	fed up *(with)*
	jillaroo	female pupil on sheep/cattle station
	joey	baby kangaroo
	Jo Blake	snake
	jumbuck/s	sheep
K	**kero/kerosene**	paraffin
	kick in	make a money contribution
	king wave	enormous, irregular wave
	Kiwi	New Zealander
	knock	deride/criticise

	AUSTRALIAN	ENGLISH
L	**lairy**	gaudy/flashy *(of clothes)*
	lamb's fry	lamb's liver
	larrikin	hooligan/ruffian
	lay-by *(v.)*	put a deposit on an article in shops, etc
	lollies	sweets
	lounge	three-piece suite
	lounge room	lounge/living room/sitting-room
	lubra	Aboriginal woman
	lurk	scheme/trick for achieving one's ends
M	**manchester**	household linen
	mark *(agric.)*	castrate
	masonite	hardboard
	metho	methylated spirits/meths
	MHR	Member of House of Representatives – Federa
	middie	drink measure

AUSTRALIAN	ENGLISH
milk bar	dairy and general grocery shop
mob	flock of sheep, etc./crowd of people
monsoon forest	rainforest
mountain ash	species of eucalypt
mozzie	mosquito
muffler *(of car, etc.)*	silencer
mulga	outback/acacia plant
Murray grey	Australian breed of cattle

N

nasho	national serviceman
nature strip	grass verge
never never	remote outback
new Australian	immigrant
no-hoper	ne'er-do-well
no standing *(road sign)*	no waiting
Noah's ark	shark
nong	idiot
no worries	that's all right/no problem

AUSTRALIAN	ENGLISH

O

odometer	mileometer/trip meter
off-sider	mate/assistant
outback	remote Australia
oval	sports field
overlander	cattle drover
overseas	abroad
OYOs *(own your own flats)*	owner-occupied flats
Oz	Australia

P

paddock	field
paddy melon	small field melon
paddy melon/pademelon	small wallaby
pads	cowpats
parka	anorak
pastoralist	farmer *(on large cattle property with pastoral lease)*
pedestrian crossing	
flashing light	Belisha beacon
pick *(v.)*	spot-identify

play possum	pretend to be dead/asleep/ignorant
pom/pommy	English person
pony	drink measure
port	suitcase
postie	postman
pot	medium-sized glass of beer
prang	bump/knock *(especially cars)*
Premier	head of an Australian State
Prime Minister	Australian Federal Prime Minister
public holiday	bank holiday
Public Service	Civil Service

R

rapt *(in something)*	keen on something
rapt	delighted/enraptured
ratbag	rascal
reggo	registration of car, etc.
rest room	public toilet
ringer	stockman
rip *(tow)*	dangerous offshore current

AUSTRALIAN	ENGLISH
road train	long-distance lorry with several trailers
rock melon	cantaloup melon
roo	kangaroo
rouseabout	farm labourer
rover	field position in Aussie Rules
rubbedy *(derived from rub-a-dub-dub)*	pub
rubbish *(v.)*	put down
rubbish tin	waste-paper basket
ruckman	field position in Aussie Rules
run *(for election)*	stand *(for election)*
rugged up	wrapped up against the cold
runners *(shoes)*	trainers

S

saltbush	bush found in arid areas
salvo	member of Salvation Army
sand groper *(colloq.)*	West Australian
sand shoes	plimsolls/gym shoes

AUSTRALIAN	ENGLISH
schooner	large beer glass
scone *(off one's)*	head
sea wasp	lethal jelly fish
sealed *(road)*	tarmac surfaced road
sedan	saloon car
semi- *(trailer)*	articulated lorry
shallots	spring onions
sheila	girl/woman
shootin' through *(like a Bondi tram)*	to leave/not stopping/in a hurry
shout *(v. and n.)*	buy a round of drinks
singlet	vest
skite/skiter	boast/boaster
skivvy	polo-neck top
slack	lazy
sleepout	extension to a house/enclosed verandah
sling *(n.)*	underhand commission
sling off *(v.)*	deride/slag off

AUSTRALIAN	ENGLISH
slygrogging	illicit drinking
smoke-o	tea-break
smokes	fags/cigarettes
snag	sausage
snaky	irritable/touchy/angry
spinifax	rough, spiny grass
sport *(colloq.)*	mate/pal/old man
squatter *(early settlement period)*	person who occupied and fenced open land
station	large sheep or cattle farm
station wagon/wagon	estate car
stinger	lethal jellyfish
stock route	track for droving cattle *(being replaced by beef roads qv)*
stockyard	cattle pen
stretcher	camp bed
strides	men's trousers
stroller	pushchair

AUSTRALIAN	ENGLISH
stubby	small, squat beer bottle/pair of shorts
sunbake	sunbathe
sundowner	happy hour
supper	late evening snack
surfies	surfers
swag	bundle of belongings/sleeping gear
Sydneysider	Sydney resident

T

AUSTRALIAN	ENGLISH
tank *(in the bush)*	water storage in dry areas
Tassie	Tasmania
taxi-truck	van hire service
teller *(in a bank)*	cashier
Territorian	inhabitant of the Northern Territory
thingo	thing/thingummy
thongs	flip-flops
tinny	can of beer
tow-truck	breakdown vehicle
track *(the)*	Alice Springs–Darwin Road

AUSTRALIAN	ENGLISH
truck *(n.)*	lorry
truck *(v.)*	carry by lorry
tube	can *(of beer)*
tucker	food
turkey's nest	dam
two-up	illegal gambling game

U

underground mutton	rabbit *(meal)*
ute/utility	single-cab truck

V

vest	waistcoat/sleeveless knitted pullover
vintage *(n.)*	a mature wine

W

wait on	wait for
walkabout	lengthy walk to get away from it all
welter	habit/over-do something

AUSTRALIAN	ENGLISH
wet *(the)*	rainy season in the Tropics
wharfie	docker
willy-willy	cyclone/tropical dust-storm
winery	vineyard
within cooee of	within shouting distance/no distance at all
wog	bug/virus/disease
woolgrower	sheepfarmer
woomera *(Aboriginal)*	spear-launching device
wowser	spoilsport/puritan
zucchini	courgettes

Z

IDIOMS

Australian	English
Someone who doesn't let the moths out of his wallet	A tight-fisted person
Rafferty's Rules	Anything goes
Beyond the rabbit-proof fence	At the back of beyond
She's sweet/she's apples/she'll be right	Everything's O.K.
Get into second gear/rattle your dags	Get a move on
Go for your life	Go ahead
Home and hosed	In the bag
Am I ever!	Not half!
A one pot screamer	Weak-headed/someone who can't hold drink
Spit the dummy	Throw in the sponge/give in
A bunch of fives	To square up/threaten with fist
Two spits and a jump	Within spitting distance
Don't come the raw prawn	You can't fool me

ENGLISH—AUSTRALIAN

	ENGLISH	AUSTRALIAN
A	**Aboriginal woman**	gin/lubra
	abroad	overseas
	afternoon	arvo
	anorak	parka
	articulated lorry	semi- *(trailer)*
	asbestos board	fibro
	Australia/Australian	Aussie/Oz
	Australian Rules – football	Aussie Rules/footy
	Australian soldier	Anzac/digger
B	**back garden**	back yard
	back of beyond	back of Bourke/beyond the black stump
	bank holiday	public holiday
	beer glass *(large)*	schooner
	Belisha beacon	flashing light at pedestrian crossing
	boast/boaster	skite/skiter

ENGLISH	AUSTRALIAN
breakdown vehicle	tow-truck
B.B.C.	British Broadcasting Corporation
bug/virus/disease	wog
bulb *(light)*	globe
bump/knock *(especially cars)*	prang
bungalow	single-storey house
buy a round of drinks	shout *(v.)*

C

ENGLISH	AUSTRALIAN
camp bed	stretcher
cantaloup melon	rock melon
cashier *(in a bank)*	teller
cattle drover	overlander
cattle pen	stockyard
central Australia	the Centre
certainty/safe thing	dead cert
Civil Service	Public Service
clothes *(best)*	duds

ENGLISH	AUSTRALIAN
Commonwealth *(usually the British Commonwealth)*	Commonwealth *(usually the Commonwealth of Australia)*
compensation	compo
conscription	draft
contribute *(money)*	kick in
countryside	the bush
courgettes	zucchini
crayon	coloured pencil
criticise/deride	rubbish/knock
curtains	drapes

D

deposit *(to put down a)*	lay-by
delighted/enraptured	rapt
deride	rubbish *(v.)*
die	pass in one's check
docker	wharfie
drunk	full
Durex *(brand name)*/condoms	contraceptive

	ENGLISH	AUSTRALIAN
E	**English person**	Pom/Pommy
	estate car	station wagon/wagon
	eucalyptus	gum tree/eucalypt
	extension *(extra room built on to house)*	sleepout
F	**farmer**	grazier/pastoralist
	fed up *(with)*	jacked *(off)*
	field	paddock
	fire hydrant	fire plug
	flipflops	thongs
	food	tucker
	frankfurters	frankfurts
	fire	heater
G	**galvanised iron**	galvo
	girl/woman	sheila
	give up	give away
	good/excellent	bonzer

	ENGLISH	AUSTRALIAN
	grass verge	nature strip
	great/marvellous	beaut(y)
	grocer	general store

ENGLISH	AUSTRALIAN
habit	welter
hardboard	masonite
herd *(of cattle, etc.)*	mob
highwayman	bushranger
hiker	bushwalker
honest	dinkum/fair dinkum
hooligan	larrikin
horse	moke
horse *(wild)*	brumby
hot-water bottle	hot-water bag
household linen	manchester

ENGLISH	AUSTRALIAN
ice lolly	icy pole
idiot	galah/nong/dill
illicit drinking	slygrogging

	ENGLISH	AUSTRALIAN
	immersion heater	hot-water service
	irritable/touchy/angry	snaky
J	**jellyfish** *(lethal)*	Sea wasp/stinger
	jersey/sports shirt	guernsey
	junction *(road)*	intersection
K	**kangaroo** *(baby)*	joey
	kangaroo *(large/anything big)*	boomer
	keen *(on something)*	rapt *(in something)*
L	**lamb's liver**	lamb's fry
	lay-by *(n.)*	parking bay
	limited *(company)*/plc	incorporated
	look *(have a)*	have a Captain Cook
	lorry	truck
	lost	bushed
	lounge/living-room	lounge room

	ENGLISH	AUSTRALIAN
M	mate/assistant	off-sider
	methylated spirits/meths	metho
	mileometer	odometer
	motorway	freeway
	M.P.	member of Parliament
	mythical creature	bunyip
N	national serviceman	nasho
	native Australian	Aborigine
	ne'er-do-well	no hoper
	New Zealander	Kiwi
	No Waiting *(road sign)*	No Standing
O	off-licence	bottle shop
	outhouse	outside toilet
	owner occupied flats	OYO's *(own your own flats)*
P	paid up/solvent/in the black	financial
	paintwork *(on cars, etc.)*	duco
	paraffin	kerosene/kero

ENGLISH	AUSTRALIAN
Parliament *(House of Commons)*	House of Representatives *(Federal)*
Parliament *(House of Lords)*	The Senate *(Federal)*
petrol pump	bowser
plimsolls/gym shoes	sand shoes
plot *(of land)*	block of land
pond/reservoir *(man-made)*	dam
pond *(natural)*	billabong
postman	postie
pub	rubbedy/hotel
pushchair	stroller

Q

Queenslander	Banana-bender *(colloq.)*

R

rainforest	monsoon forest
rake-off *(n.)*	sling
rascal	ratbag

ENGLISH	AUSTRALIAN
registration *(of car)*	reggo
remote Australia	outback
remote country	backblocks
ring/call	bell *(give someone a)*
round of drinks *(to buy)*	shout *(v. and n.)*
saloon car	sedan
Salvation Army *(member of)*	Salvo
scared/the creeps	the Jimmy Britts
schooner	large sherry glass
sellotape	durex/sticky tape
shanty/shack	humpy
shark meat	flake
sheep	jumbuck/s
sheep farmer	woolgrower
shouting distance *(no distance at all)*	within cooee of
sick/ill/out of order	crook
silencer	muffler

S

ENGLISH	AUSTRALIAN
South Australian	crow eater *(colloq.)*
spitting image of	dead ringer for
spoilsport	wowser
sportsfield	oval
spot/identity	pick
spring onions	shallots
squatter	unauthorised occupier of property
stag party	buck's party/buck's night
stand *(for election)*	run *(for election)*
storm flood	flash-flood
stream *(occasional)*	creek
suitcase	port
sunbathe	sunbake
supper	dinner
support *(sports)*	barrack for
sweets	lollies
swim suit	bathers/cozzy

	ENGLISH	AUSTRALIAN

T

tarmac-surfaced road	sealed road
Tasmanian resident	Apple-islander *(colloq.)*
tea-break	smoke-o
thing/thingummy	thingo
toilet *(public)*	rest room/comfort station
trainers *(shoes)*	runners
trick/scheme	lurk
trouble	strife
turn out right	come good

U

unlicensed restaurant	BYO *(bring your own)* restaurant/party
unmetalled road	gravel road

V

van-hire service	taxi-truck
vest	singlet
vineyard	winery
vomit *(v.)*	chunder

W

ENGLISH	AUSTRALIAN
wait for	wait on
wallaby *(small)*	pademelon/paddy melon
walk *(lengthy, to get away from it all)*	walkabout
waste-paper basket	rubbish tin
well done/good for you	good on you
wellingtons	gum boots
West Australian	sand groper *(colloq.)*
whirlwind	willy-willy
wine *(mature)*	vintage *(n.)*
wrapped up *(against the cold)*	rugged up
worthless	clapped out
worthless person/idiot	drongo

ENGLISH	AUSTRALIAN
IDIOMS	
A tight-fisted person	Someone who doesn't let the moths out of his wallet
Anything goes	Rafferty's Rules
At the back of beyond	Beyond the rabbit-proof fence
Everything's O.K.	She's sweet/she's apples/she'll be right
Get a move on	Get into second-gear/rattle your dags
Go ahead	Go for your life
In the bag	Home and hosed
Not half!	Am I ever!
Weak-headed/someone who can't hold their drink	A one pot screamer
Throw in the sponge/give in	Spit the dummy
To square up/threaten with fist	A bunch of fives
Within spitting distance	Two spits and a jump
You can't fool me	Don't come the raw prawn

OTHER TITLES AVAILABLE

Language Glossaries

American English/English American
Australian English/English Australian
Irish English/English Irish
Gay Slang
Geordie English
Lancashire English
Prison Slang
Rhyming Cockney Slang
Scouse English
Yiddish English/English Yiddish
Scottish English/English Scottish
Yorkshire English
Ultimate Language of Flowers
Hip Hop English
Rude Rhyming Slang
Military Slang

Literary Quiz & Puzzle Books

Jane Austen
Brontë Sisters
Charles Dickens
Gilbert & Sullivan
Thomas Hardy
Sherlock Holmes
Shakespeare

The Death of Kings (A medical history
of the Kings & Queens of England)

Abson Books London
5 Sidney Square London E1 2EY
Tel 020 7790 4737 Fax 020 7790 7346
email absonbooks@aol.com
Web: www.absonbooks.co.uk

NOTES: USE THIS PAGE FOR YOUR OWN FAVOURITE 'STRINE'.